IN THE JUNGLE

COLORING BOOK

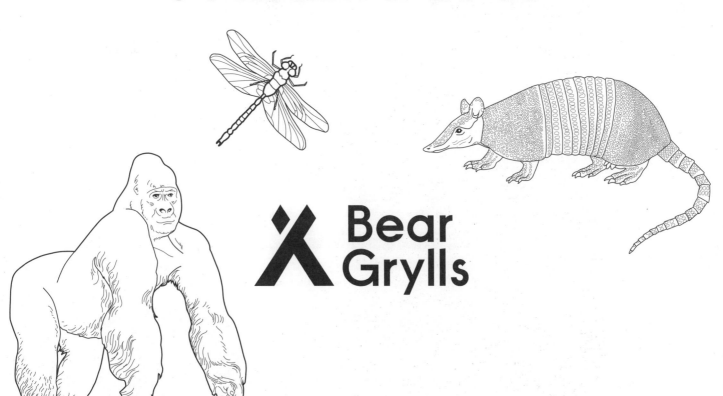

Bear
Grylls

 **Bear Grylls**

I've been lucky enough to visit some of the most remote and inhospitable jungles on the planet—and I survived!

Jungles are incredible places for adventuring and learning about wildlife because they are teeming with mind-blowing plant and animal species. Through my encounters with deadly snakes, venomous spiders, and terrifying crocs in jungles around the world, I've learned how important it is to understand as much as we can about wildlife if we are to help protect it. Every animal in the jungle has a critical part to play in nature, from the humble termite and dragonfly, right up to the biggest elephant.

In this book, you'll not only get to color in amazing jungle creatures, you'll also learn some fascinating facts about them along the way. Enjoy the adventure!

SLOW LORIS

BEAR SAYS

Slow lorises drink nectar using their long tongues. Out of all the primates, they have the longest tongues.

HABITAT

DIET

Fruit, insects, frogs, eggs, small reptiles

Did you know that "loris" is a Dutch word meaning "clown"? They have clown-like features, including large eyes and black patches around their eyes.

SIZE

8 in.

ARMADILLO

BEAR SAYS

Can you roll up into a ball like an armadillo? It's an amazing trick that can save their lives. Only one type of these shelled critters can do it— the three-banded armadillo.

HABITAT

Armadillo means "the little armored one" in Spanish. Their hard shells help protect them from being eaten by predators.

DIET

Fruit, insects, remains of dead animals

SIZE

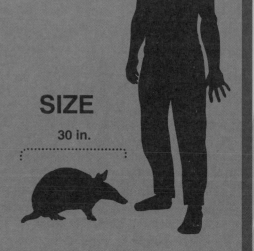

30 in.

TOUCAN

BEAR SAYS

I've had lots of adventures in the jungle. If you look up you can see colorful butterflies and birds flying. But did you know that toucans aren't good at flying?

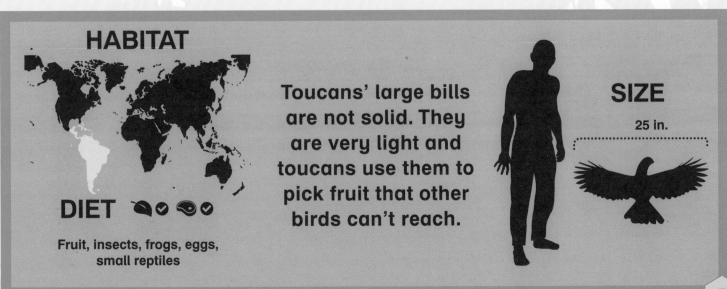

HABITAT

DIET
Fruit, insects, frogs, eggs, small reptiles

Toucans' large bills are not solid. They are very light and toucans use them to pick fruit that other birds can't reach.

SIZE
25 in.

SLOTH

BEAR SAYS

I can camouflage myself by painting my face green and wearing khaki clothes. Sloths have a natural camouflage—algae. They move so slowly that it grows on their fur!

HABITAT

DIET
Leaves, shoots, fruit, occasionally insects and rodents

Sloths are very slow! It can take them up to one month to digest a meal, and they only go to the bathroom once a week.

SIZE
24 in.

MACAWS

BEAR SAYS

I have eaten and drunk many strange things, such as liquid from elephant poop and fruit from bear poop. Macaws eat clay to help them flush the poisonous seeds they eat out of their body.

HABITAT

DIET

Fruit, seeds, nuts

Macaws have very strong beaks. They also have a bone inside their tongue that helps them open hard nut shells and seed pods.

SIZE

4 ft.

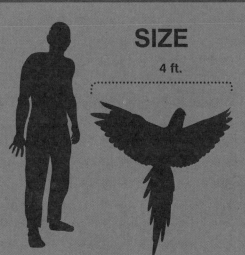

TIGERS

BEAR SAYS

Tigers are excellent hunters. They
have very good eyesight, they can
run up to 40 mph, and can jump
distances of more than
20 ft.! That's as long as three fully
grown men!

HABITAT

DIET

Wild pigs, birds, fish, monkeys

The tiger is the largest species in the big cat family. Unlike most other big cats, they are excellent swimmers.

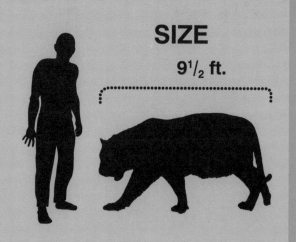

SIZE

9½ ft.

FOREST ELEPHANTS

BEAR SAYS

Forest elephants communicate over long distances by sending out a rumbling sound that is too low for humans to hear!

HABITAT

African forest elephants live in African rain forests in big family groups.

SIZE

8 ft.

DIET

Leaves, fruit, bark

PIT VIPER

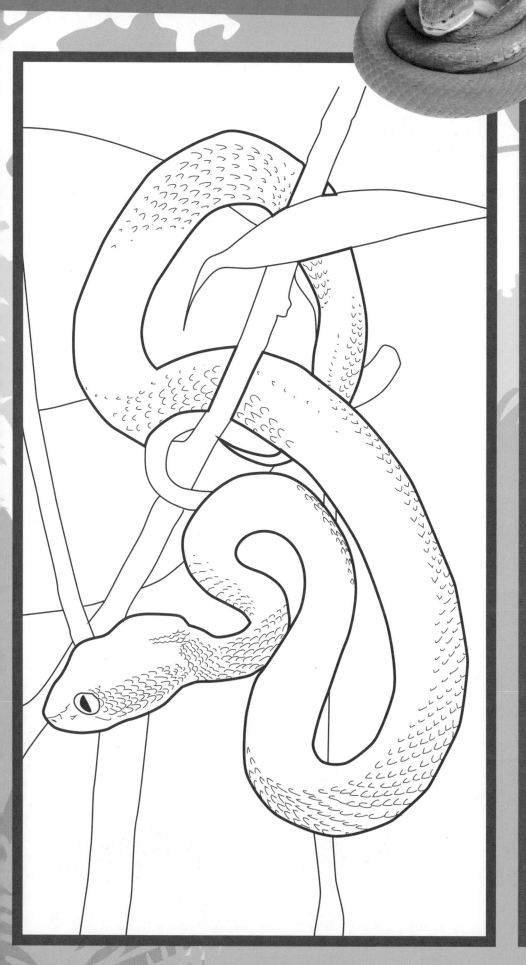

HABITAT

DIET

Mice, rats, lizards, birds, frogs

Pit vipers have the special ability to sense heat from their prey—this makes them really good at hunting at night.

SIZE

18 in.

BUTTERFLIES

A butterfly's life begins as a very tiny egg laid on a leaf. From this develops a larva—the butterfly's caterpillar stage. Eventually, the larva makes a cocoon or chrysalis. Safe inside, the larva develops into a pupa. Finally, a beautiful butterfly is released from this container. What an amazing transformation!

Some butterflies are brightly colored, but others, like this cracker butterfly from Peru, find it more useful to be able to blend into the background. Can you spot it?

Try coloring in the picture on the right—see if you can achieve the same effect!

BEAR SAYS

Butterflies don't taste with their tongues—they taste with their feet! They don't have mouths to bite and chew food—they have a straw-like structure that they use to drink nectar.

GORILLA

HABITAT

SIZE

5¹/₂ ft.

Gorillas are the world's largest primate. They share 98 percent of their DNA with humans.

DIET

Fruit, leaves, seeds, stems

ORANGUTANS

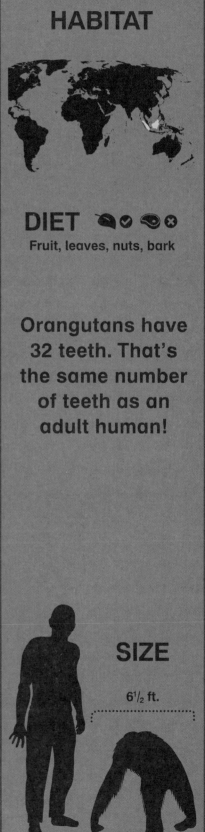

HABITAT

DIET
Fruit, leaves, nuts, bark

Orangutans have 32 teeth. That's the same number of teeth as an adult human!

SIZE

6½ ft.

IN THE CANOPY

In the rain forest, most of the plant and animal life can be found in the canopy. The canopy (which can be more than 100 feet above the forest floor) is made of branches, leaves, and vines. Most of the animals that live in the canopy fly, glide, or jump from tree to tree. You will see birds, monkeys, lizards, insects, sloths, and much more in the canopy!

FROGS

BEAR SAYS

Poison dart frogs got their name because hunters would dip their arrows in the venom of the golden poison dart frog.

HABITAT

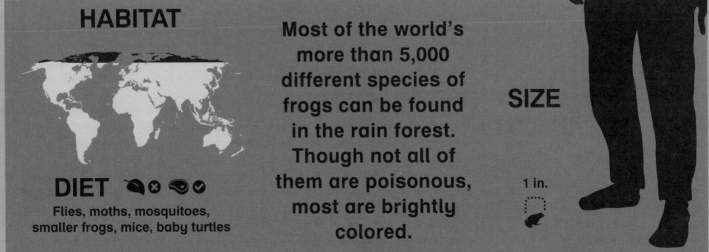

DIET

Flies, moths, mosquitoes, smaller frogs, mice, baby turtles

Most of the world's more than 5,000 different species of frogs can be found in the rain forest. Though not all of them are poisonous, most are brightly colored.

SIZE

1 in.

TERMITES

HABITAT

DIET
Dead plants, wood, cotton

Termites feed on dead plants and dead trees, as well as the wood in soil—and in houses! They play a really important part in the circle of jungle life.

SIZE

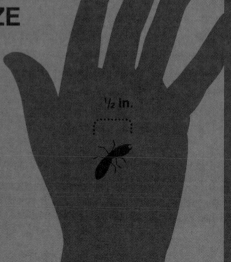

¹/₂ in.

PIRANHAS

HABITAT

DIET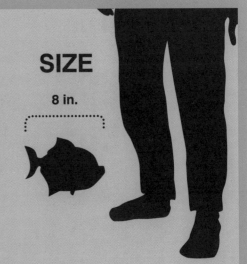
Fish, mollusks, insects

Piranhas can make three different noises: they make a sound like a bark, one like a thud, and another that sounds exactly like a drumbeat!

SIZE
8 in.

ANACONDA

HABITAT

DIET

Pigs, deer, birds, turtles, other reptiles

Anacondas kill their prey by wrapping their muscular bodies around it and squeezing until it can't breathe. Then the anaconda swallows it whole!

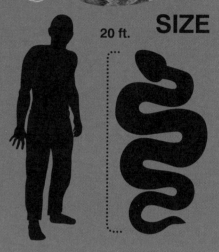

SIZE

20 ft.

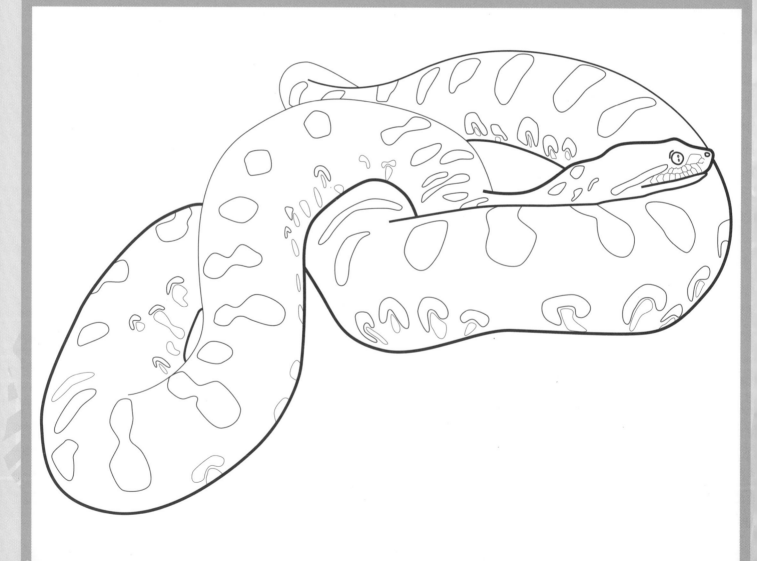

HUMMINGBIRDS

BEAR SAYS

Hummingbirds beat their wings really fast, which uses up a lot of energy. At night, they save their energy by going into a "torpor," a type of deep sleep.

HABITAT

DIET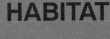

Flower nectar, tree sap, insects, pollen

There are more than 320 different species of hummingbird. The smallest hummingbird is the tiny bee hummingbird. It is the smallest bird in the world!

SIZE

3¹/₂ in.

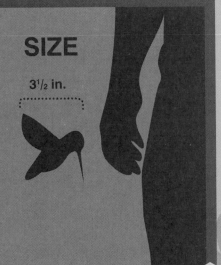

JAGUAR

HABITAT

DIET

Birds, eggs, crocodiles, snakes, deer

Jaguars are excellent at climbing and they like to live alone. They mark their territory with pee and by scraping trees.

SIZE

6 ft.

BEAR SAYS

Jaguars sometimes wiggle their tails over water as a lure to catch fish!

TAPIRS

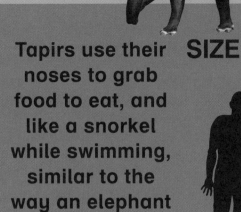

BEAR SAYS

The seeds that tapirs eat come out in their poop. This acts as a fertilizer and helps new plants to grow on the forest floor.

HABITAT

DIET
Water plants, fruit, buds, twigs, leaves

Tapirs use their noses to grab food to eat, and like a snorkel while swimming, similar to the way an elephant uses its trunk!

SIZE

3 ft.

FOREST FLOOR

The forest floor is where you will find all of the biggest animals in the rain forest, like elephants, gorillas, tapirs, tigers, jaguars, and more. It is also where the trees get all of their food. Dead plants and animals decompose on the forest floor, and the nutrients are recycled into the earth. The bugs that live on the forest floor help with this by breaking down the dead plants and animals. How many animals can you spot on the forest floor?

SPIDER

BEAR SAYS

Golden orb weaver spiders build impressive webs. If there is a strong wind, they make a hole in the web so the wind can blow through it without breaking it.

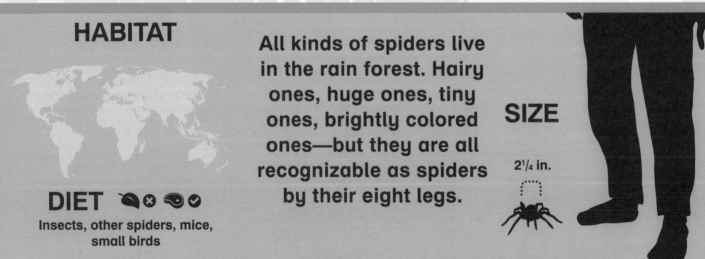

HABITAT

All kinds of spiders live in the rain forest. Hairy ones, huge ones, tiny ones, brightly colored ones—but they are all recognizable as spiders by their eight legs.

DIET Insects, other spiders, mice, small birds

SIZE

2¼ in.

SQUIRREL MONKEYS

BEAR SAYS

Squirrel monkeys live in families called "troops." There are usually about 50 members of the family, but a troop can be as large as 500 monkeys!

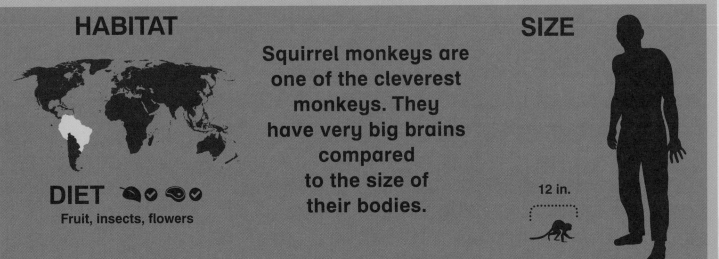

HABITAT

DIET
Fruit, insects, flowers

Squirrel monkeys are one of the cleverest monkeys. They have very big brains compared to the size of their bodies.

SIZE

12 in.

IN THE RIVER

Jungle rivers and the areas around them are home to many different animals. Some animals live in the river, like eels, alligators, and fish, while others, such as tigers, birds, and snakes, visit it every day, either for water or to hunt the animals that live in and around it. There are more than 3,000 species of fish that we know about living in the Amazon River alone.

DRAGONFLIES

BEAR SAYS

Dragonflies have two pairs of wings that allow them to turn easily in the air, hover, and fly backward—just like a helicopter!

HABITAT

SIZE

Dragonflies don't have a long lifespan —most only live for a few weeks with their wings.

2 in.

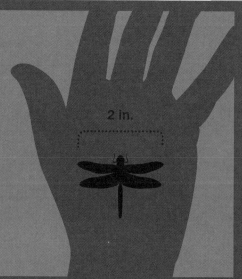

DIET

Mosquitoes, butterflies, moths, bees, ants, smaller dragonflies